HIDDEN CODE OF MARKETING

HIDDEN CODE OF MARKETING

SECRET SCIENCE BEHIND EVERY SUCCESSFUL MARKETING MESSAGE

P. SHARMA

AXEMAN

Fair Use Notice

ISBN13: 978-93-47026-26-3 (Ebook Edition)
ISBN13: 978-93-47026-42-3 (Paperback Edition)
ISBN13: 978-93-47026-73-7 (Hardcover Edition)

DEDICATION

To my family, friends, and team -- You helped me gain the skills and confidence necessary to write this book. You also provided constant inspiration and support throughout the entire process. Thanks for your support!

UNLOCK THE CODE BEHIND HIGH-IMPACT MARKETING

YOUR FREE BONUSES ARE WAITING!

Most marketing doesn't fail due to lack of effort. It fails because it ignores how people actually think.

By reading Hidden Code of Marketing, you've taken a step toward understanding what drives attention, trust, and action.

To help you apply these ideas right away, I've created a set of free bonus resources. Inside you'll find a workbook, website audit manual, campaign checklist, and an AI manual. Each resource is practical, simple, and designed for real-world use.

This is my thank-you for reading the book.

Visit

leadspanda.com/bonuses

and start building messages that feel more human.

AI Manual | **Checklist** | **Website Audit Manual** | **Workbook**

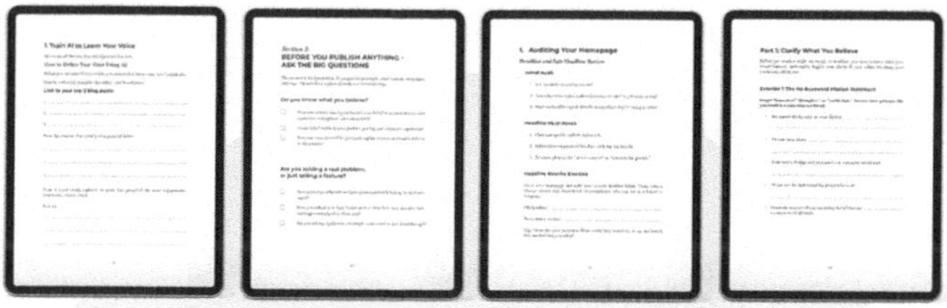

CONTENTS

Introduction xi

1. Why Authenticity Became Non-Negotiable 1
How Trust Collapsed and What Marketers Must Do Now
2. What Authenticity Actually Means 7
Clarity, Consistency, and Congruence Explained
3. The Psychology of Trust 21
Why the Human Brain Rewards Honest Marketing
4. How to Make Your Brand More Authentic 31
Practical Ways to Be Real, Without Losing Sales
5. Authentic Funnels That Convert 41
Emails, Ads, and Pages People Trust
6. Keeping It Real in the Age of AI 55
Using Automation Without Losing Your Voice
7. The ROI of Being Real 63
How Authenticity Drives Growth and Profit

Be Real, or Be Forgotten 75
Now Take Action 81
Thank You for Reading My Book 83
Get Expert Help with Your Brand Story 85
Notes 87
Acknowledgment 91
About the Author 93
Other Books You Might Like 95

INTRODUCTION

WHY HONESTY, TRUST, AND TRUTH NOW DRIVE MARKETING

Let's start with a pizza.

Not a metaphorical one. An actual, cheesy, doughy, greasy pizza, the kind millions of Americans ordered from Domino's in the mid 2000s.

Only… no one liked it.

The feedback from customers was nothing short of blunt[1].

"Tastes like cardboard."

"Ketchup on crust."

"Microwave pizza is better."

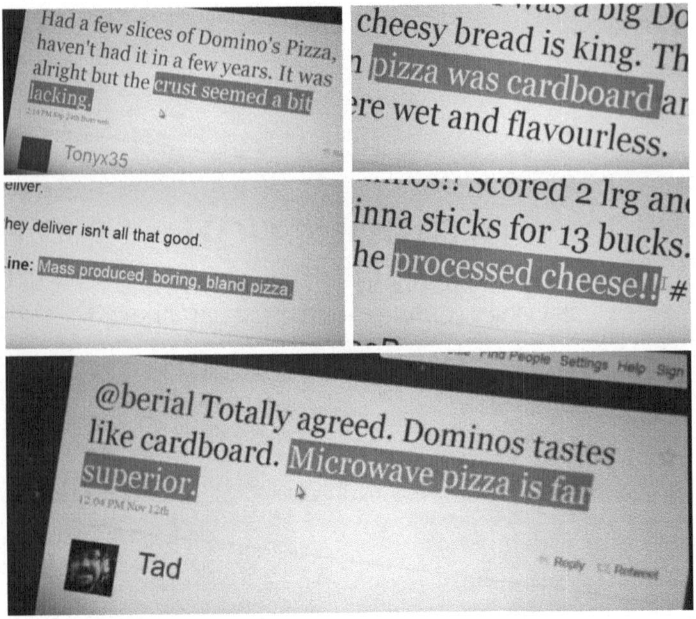

FIGURE 1: Screenshots of reviews by customers for the Domino's Pizza

Domino's faced a barrage of harsh criticisms online, questioning the taste of their pizza.

And these weren't one-off comments. It was a full-blown reputation crisis. Domino's wasn't just losing market share, but they were becoming a punchline.

Now, imagine you're in charge of their marketing. What would you do?

May be slap a new sticker on the box? Hire an influencer or two? Distract people with a limited-time offer or bundle deal?

This has been the go-to strategy of many brands: *change the subject.*

But Domino's did the opposite. In 2010, they launched a national campaign called "The Pizza Turnaround."

It wasn't a joke. It wasn't spin. It was raw, brutally honest, and for the time, authentic!

They showed real customers trashing the product. They showed their chefs reading the hate mail. They released footage[2] of actual focus group discussions with participants dishing out their no-holds-barred criticisms.

They admitted the crust was awful. And they said, flat-out: "We're sorry. We're fixing it."

Then they did something even more important: they changed the recipe.

They re-engineered the dough, revamped the sauce, and overhauled their kitchens. With boxes containing their new and improved pizzas in tow, they visited the homes of their fiercest detractors to get their feedback.

The results?

A 14.3% increase in same-store sales, the biggest jump in company history.

Over the next decade, Domino's went from fast-food failure to Wall Street darling. Domino's stock rose from single-digit levels in 2009 to several hundred dollars per share over the following decade.

All because they did the one thing most companies are terrified to do:

They told the truth.

WELCOME TO THE AGE OF NO BULLSH*T

That Domino's moment wasn't just good PR. It was a strategic decision, and a profitable one.

It tapped into something powerful that most digital marketers today still don't fully grasp:

Authenticity sells.

Not in a vague, "be yourself" kind of way. But in a

bottom-line, track-the-revenue, people-will-actually-buy-from-you kind of way.

When Domino's told the truth, they didn't lose customers; they gained trust.

When they showed their flaws, people leaned in, not away.

When they owned their mistakes, their brand became… human.

And in an age of spammy email, fake scarcity, and AI-generated copy, being human is the greatest competitive advantage you have. And you've got to hang on to that.

Real Stories Drive Real Results

Let's be honest. Most marketing today feels like it was written by a robot pretending to be a guru and offering to make people's problems disappear with a wave of a magic wand or grant their wishes.

Everyone's promising "massive results." Everyone's "crushing it." And somehow, every business is both "revolutionary" and "just like you."

You know what's missing? A pulse.

Marketing has become mechanical. Overoptimized. Formulaic. Somewhere along the way, we started thinking that success was about cracking an algorithm instead of connecting with actual people.

This book is here to say: Maybe it's time to change that.

It's time to bring marketing back to what it was meant to be, which is honest, human, and effective.

That's what authenticity is. And that's what this book is about.

WHAT YOU'LL LEARN ABOUT AUTHENTICITY

We're not going to talk about vibes and vision boards. This isn't a soft book full of branding platitudes and Instagram quotes.

You're going to learn how to use authenticity as a strategy.

We'll cover:

- Why consumers are done with hype (and what they trust instead)
- The psychology behind why honesty converts better than cleverness
- How to build trust into every part of your digital marketing, from your homepage to your headlines to your funnels
- What real authenticity looks like (hint: it's not crying on camera)
- How to be honest without oversharing, overselling, or tanking your message
- Why telling the truth makes your marketing faster, easier, and more scalable

And yes, we'll talk about sales. This book won't just make you feel good about being authentic. It'll help you make money doing it.

Because when people trust you, they don't need convincing.

They click faster, they buy faster, they come back more often.

THE BIG PROBLEM: TRUST IS BROKEN

Here's the harsh truth: people don't believe marketers anymore.

They don't trust ads. They don't trust influencers. They don't trust "limited time" countdown timers.

Years of bait-and-switch tactics, overhyped claims, and fake urgency have burned them out.

Today's buyers have industrial-strength BS detectors. They can smell insincerity from a mile away. And when they sense you're full of it, they're gone.

The funny (or not so funny) thing is, even digital marketers feel like what they're doing is deceiving people. A quick Reddit search[3] for "marketing scam" will reveal dozens of posts from marketers. Here's a good example:

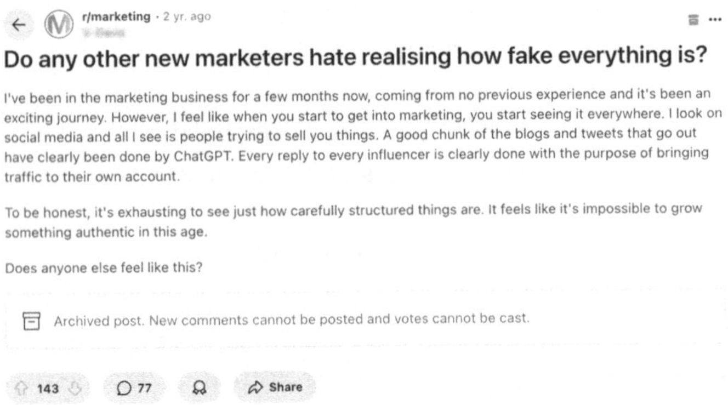

FIGURE 2: Even marketers are feeling that the age-old systems of selling things to people are starting to feel like a scam

This isn't just a branding issue. It's a conversion issue. It's a revenue issue. It's a business-threatening issue.

If you don't have trust, you don't have traction. Period.

THE GOOD NEWS: THE BAR HAS NEVER BEEN LOWER

You don't have to be the funniest brand in your niche. Or the most creative. Or the cheapest.

You just have to be real, consistent, visible, and confident.

In fact, in a world drowning in hype, truth becomes a novelty.

When your message rings true, it cuts through. People remember it. They talk about it. They act on it.

And they come back, because they trust that you'll deliver again.

SHOULD YOU CONTINUE READING?

This book is for you if:

- You're tired of manipulative marketing tactics that don't even work
- You're struggling to connect with your audience in a meaningful way
- You've built a good product or service, but don't know how to sell it without feeling fake
- You believe business should feel honest, but you still want to win

Whether you're a solopreneur, a marketing lead, a small business owner, or a copywriter trying to write with more punch and less pretense, this book is your permission slip to stop pretending.

And your playbook for what to do instead.

REAL MARKETING IS BRAVE MARKETING

Being real in your marketing takes guts.

It's easier to follow a script. It's safer to blend in. It's tempting to chase whatever trend is working on TikTok this week.

But the real wins, the loyal customers, the word-of-mouth referrals, the raving fans, come from realness.

Authenticity isn't a weakness. It's not passivity. It's not "just being nice."

It's clarity. Confidence. Leadership.

People are desperate for something that feels real. Something they can trust. Something that means it.

You don't need to be louder. You need to be more you.

READY TO BE REAL?

Domino's isn't the only brand that turned things around by telling the truth. You'll see more stories like theirs throughout this book. Not just because they're entertaining, but because they prove a point:

Authenticity isn't a luxury. It's a strategy.

And it's the most powerful one you've got.

So if you're ready to ditch the digital mask and start marketing like someone people want to buy from, let's begin.

CHAPTER 1
WHY AUTHENTICITY BECAME NON-NEGOTIABLE
HOW TRUST COLLAPSED AND WHAT MARKETERS MUST DO NOW

THE DAY PEPSI AND BURGER KING FORGOT TO BE HUMAN

In April 2017, Pepsi released an ad[1] featuring Kendall Jenner joining a protest and handing a can of Pepsi to a police officer. The campaign was intended to signal unity and optimism during a period of global unrest.

Instead, it quickly became one of the most criticized marketing missteps of the decade. Viewers felt the ad oversimplified real-world protest movements. It also reduced deeply rooted social justice issues to a feel-good branding moment, unintentionally trivializing experiences that were still raw and unresolved for many communities. Pepsi pulled the ad within 24 hours and issued a public apology.

This wasn't just a PR failure; it was a warning shot.

The world had changed. Consumers weren't interested in polished platitudes or feel-good narratives that rang hollow. They wanted something real. They wanted brands to reflect values, not manipulate them. Pepsi's mistake wasn't just poor taste; it was poor reading of the cultural moment. And in the digital era, that misreading comes at a steep price.

A few years later, Burger King fell into a similar trap.

In 2021, on International Women's Day, the fast food chain tweeted[2]: "Women belong in the kitchen."

FIGURE 3: What was meant to be a message of women's empowerment sparked a conflagration of anti-feminist backlash for the international fast food chain brand Burger King

The intention was to draw attention to gender disparity in the culinary field and announce a scholarship program. But in isolation, and especially as a tweet, it backfired. The backlash overshadowed the initiative entirely. Once again, the attempt to be edgy came across as tone-deaf. Apologies followed. Trust eroded.

The lesson repeated itself: being clever without being authentic is a dangerous game.

THE COLLAPSE OF TRUST

Today, brands operate in a world where trust is not only fragile, but it's at an all-time low. According to the Edelman Special Report[3], only 26% of consumers listen to what a brand says in its advertising. Think about that. Almost two-thirds of your audience approaches your messaging with skepticism or outright disbelief.

In the same report, 81% of consumers say they need to trust a brand before they'll buy from it. Not want. Not prefer. Need. It's the starting line now, not the finish.

In a 2023 Edelman report, 51% of those who were surveyed[4] said that they will disengage from a brand due to inauthenticity.

These aren't just soft signals. Trust has become the currency of the digital age. It determines whether your audience listens, engages, buys, or walks away.

THE TRANSPARENCY GENERATION

Modern audiences, especially Millennials and Gen Z, have grown up in a digital world where they can fact-check claims in seconds, call out inconsistencies publicly, and reward brands that feel human.

According to the same 2023 Edelam report, 64% of millennials and 64% of Gen Z say brand authenticity is important when choosing which brands to support. This isn't a fringe mindset. It's a mainstream expectation.

EConsumers overall say authenticity matters when deciding what brands they like and support, and they won't have second thoughts about stopping from buying from a brand they consider inauthentic.

The implication? You might not always know when you've lost trust, but you'll feel it in your numbers.

PERFORMATIVE MARKETING IS DEAD

Performative marketing, the kind that slaps a rainbow flag on a logo in June or hashtags a cause just because it's trending, doesn't cut it anymore. People can spot a stunt from a mile away.

Worse, they resent it.

Consumers won't buy from a brand that supports causes that contradict their values. It's no longer about appearing socially conscious. It's about actually being aligned with your audience's beliefs and living those beliefs consistently.

In other words, authenticity isn't what you post. It's what you prove.

THE REAL FUNNEL: TRUST → ACTION → LOYALTY

Marketers love funnels. But here's the secret no one puts on the slide decks: trust is the real funnel.

Without trust, you never earn the click. Without trust, your copy falls flat. Without trust, you're fighting uphill and losing ground every time you push a product before proving you're credible.

Consumers who trust a brand[5] are 4x more likely to buy from it. They're also 53% more likely to be early adopters of new products and 76% more likely to recommend the brand to others, according to Edelman.

So if you're pouring money into paid ads, SEO, or

influencer campaigns, but your brand voice doesn't feel real? You're spending money on a leaky bucket.

And here's the kicker: brands seen as authentic can charge 20% more than their competitors. Why? Because people believe they're buying more than a product. They're buying values. They're buying trust.

MARKETING'S NEW MANDATE

The role of marketing used to be persuasion. Now, it's proof.

Every single time you post, write, tweet, email, or speak, the audience is listening closely, watching for cracks.

What you say must align with what you do. Your tone must match the times. Your content must feel like it came from a human, not a strategy deck. Because the second you feel fake, you lose the sale, maybe forever.

The upside? When you get it right, the rewards are enormous.

You build loyalty that ads can't buy. You earn attention without shouting. And you create a brand that doesn't just convert, but connects.

TRUST ISN'T A BONUS; IT'S THE BUY-IN

Pepsi and Burger King didn't fail because they were evil. They failed because they didn't listen. They failed because they treated people like targets instead of humans. They failed because they mistook cleverness for connection.

Authenticity isn't some fancy marketing term, it's just what people want now.

Be real, and they'll connect with you.

Try too hard, and they'll scroll right by.

CHAPTER 2
WHAT AUTHENTICITY ACTUALLY MEANS
CLARITY, CONSISTENCY, AND CONGRUENCE EXPLAINED

We throw the word "authentic" around a lot. It's on agency pitch decks. It's in the brand guidelines. It's in every third LinkedIn post about marketing trends.

But ask five people what it actually means, and you'll get five different answers.

Some think it means being raw. Others think it means sharing personal stories. Some mistake it for unfiltered rants. Others water it down into "being relatable."

Truth is, authenticity isn't a vibe. It's not a mood board. And it's definitely not an excuse for being sloppy, self-indulgent, or chaotic.

It's much more powerful and far more precise.

MORE THAN JUST A BUZZWORD

Let's start by clearing up what authenticity isn't.

It's not oversharing every emotional thought you have.

It's not filming your CEO crying into their phone.

It's not swearing in every subject line because "that's how we talk."

That might be real, sure, but authenticity isn't just about being real. It's about being aligned.

Aligned with your values.

Aligned with your voice.

Aligned with the expectations you set.

If you're a mental health app, maybe that level of rawness is right for your brand. But if you're a luxury hotel, maybe it isn't.

Authenticity is contextual. Strategic. Consistent.

You don't earn trust by dropping your guard once. You earn it by showing up the same way across every touchpoint.

And when you don't? People notice. BusinessChief report[1] said 40% of consumers will stop doing business with a brand if they feel it breaks trust. Authenticity isn't about looking honest. It's about behaving in a way that builds that trust, every time.

THE 3 C'S OF AUTHENTIC BRANDS

Let's define it:

Authenticity is clarity + consistency + congruence.

FIGURE 4: Real authenticity is the intersection of three elements: clarity, consistency and congruence.

Let's break that down.

1. Clarity

You know what your brand stands for. What you believe. What you don't. What you say yes to, and what you say no to.

Clarity means there's no confusion about who you are or what you're here to do.

Think about Notion[2], the productivity app. Their design, tone, UX, even their blog posts, they all reflect a clear philosophy: simple, flexible, thoughtful tools for thoughtful work. Nothing screams. Nothing distracts. Even their patch notes feel meditative.

FIGURE 5: Notion is a prime example of a brand that is clear on what they stand for

A quick check for clarity: If someone looked at your last 10 social posts, your homepage, and your email footer, would they all tell the same story?

2. Consistency

You sound like you, everywhere. From website to social to customer support.

Your brand doesn't feel like a different person in every email. You don't show up one way on Instagram and another in your onboarding sequence.

A great example is Mailchimp[3]. They've had a quirky, approachable voice for years, and it shows up everywhere. Even their 404 pages. Even their legal documents.

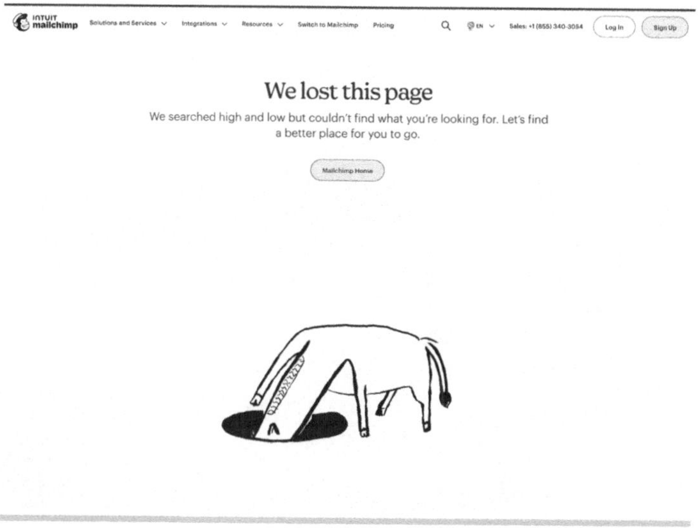

FIGURE 6: MailChimp does not leave any stone unturned when it comes to remaining consistent in communicating who they are as a brand

You don't have to guess who you're talking to.

That's consistency.

A quick check for consistency: Would a customer recognize your tone, even without your logo?

3. Congruence

You walk your talk. You act in ways that line up with your stated values. You are who you say you are.

Congruence is what most brands miss.

Saying you care about sustainability, then shipping everything in plastic? That's incongruent. Saying you put customers first, but ghosting support emails? Also incongruent.

One brand that nails this: Ben & Jerry's[4]. They've been loud and proud about their social values for decades, and they put money, product, and public pressure behind the causes they believe in. You might not agree with them, but you believe them.

FIGURE 7: Ben & Jerry's has always practiced what they preached and this authenticity has gained them a loyal customer base over the years

That's congruence.

Congruence, more than anything else, is what people look for when deciding if a brand is trustworthy. It's the alignment between what you believe internally and what you actually show externally. When those don't line up, audiences sense the disconnect instantly.

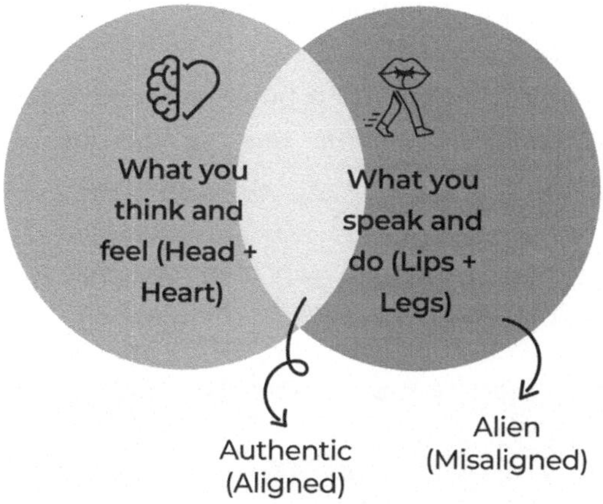

FIGURE 8: Visual representation of brand authenticity—alignment between what you think and feel (Head + Heart) and what you speak and do (Lips + Legs).

Authenticity means alignment. When what you think and feel matches what you say and do, people trust you. When it doesn't, it creates a disconnect that audiences quickly detect.

A quick check for congruence: Do your internal practices and external messaging actually match?

MORE BRANDS DOING AUTHENTICITY RIGHT

Liquid Death: Clarity on Steroids

Water in a tallboy can. That's it. That's the product.

But the brand? Completely dialed in. From the moment you see the name, you know what you're in for: irreverent humor, metal-inspired branding, a complete rejection of "clean wellness" aesthetics.

Their tagline isn't about hydration.

It's "Murder Your Thirst."

They sell water like it's a punk band. And guess what? It works. They've become one of the fastest-growing beverage brands in the U.S., and raised over $100M in funding.

The brand[5] explained why they do what they do on their About Us page:

ABOUT US

Liquid Death will not kill you. But make no mistake,
our infinitely recyclable cans of premium low-calorie beverages will absolutely murder your thirst. And it doesn't stop there. After twerking on your thirst's grave, these ruthless cans will actually donate a portion of the proceeds to help kill plastic pollution.

Why? For centuries, all the funniest and coolest
marketing and branding was only done for unhealthy products like beer, fast food, candy, and junk food.
But those days are over.

Soon, Liquid Death will use health and humor to
conquer the world and make all beverages Liquid Death
for eternity. At which point we'll finally begin turning the human race into flesh batteries to power our giant marketing robots.

FIGURE 9: Beverage brand Liquid Death is the prime example of clear and authentic marketing

That's clarity + consistency + congruence in action.

Ryanair: Consistently Petty (And Profitable)

If you've ever flown Ryanair[6], you know the drill: dirt-cheap tickets, strict baggage rules, no-frills everything.

But here's what's fascinating: their social media presence is just as brutal. They roast customers. They make memes dunking on other airlines. They are, frankly, petty.

FIGURE 10: Like them or not, Irish airline Ryanair keeps their tongue and cheek humor across all customer touch points

Their Instagram profile says: "Catch flights, not feelings."

And it works, because it's congruent.

Their brand promise is "low cost, no nonsense." And that "no nonsense" tone is baked into their Twitter feed, their app UX, and even their ads.

You might not like them, but they don't pretend to be something they're not. That's why people keep booking.

Hiut Denim: Quiet Consistency

Hiut[7] is a small UK-based denim company founded with a single mission: bring jean-making back to Cardigan, Wales.

They don't shout. They don't chase trends. Their site is quiet, minimal, and beautifully written. Their emails are thoughtful. Their jeans are expensive, and people wait months for them.

Because everything they do reinforces their one truth: We're here to make great jeans, the old way.

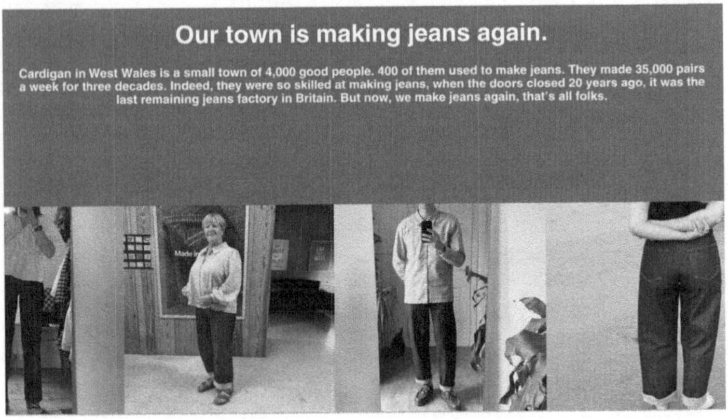

FIGURE 11: UK denim brand Hiut Denim sticks to its made-to-order business model and despite the long wait list, people continue to support them because of its inarguable consistency on how the company operates its business

They've built a global following on the back of clarity, consistency, and congruence.

Bombas: Walking the Talk

Bombas[8] isn't just selling socks. From day one, their model has been "one purchased = one donated." But they didn't stop there. They've donated over 100 million items to homeless shelters across all 50 states. Their marketing reflects this purpose, but so do their product design decisions, comfort features built specifically to meet the needs of people experiencing homelessness.

It's not charity as a campaign. It's baked into how they operate.

FIGURE 12: While many brands use philanthropy as a mere marketing tactic to attract buyers, it's the core of Bombas as a brand

That's congruence. And it's paid off. Bombas has become one of the most beloved DTC apparel brands, with a loyal customer base that buys into the mission as much as the merchandise.

That's authenticity you can feel, not just read on a label.

BRANDS THAT MISS THE MARK

Volkswagen's Emissions Scandal

Volkswagen spent years positioning itself as an eco-conscious car company. Then they were caught rigging emissions tests[9] to appear cleaner than they actually were.

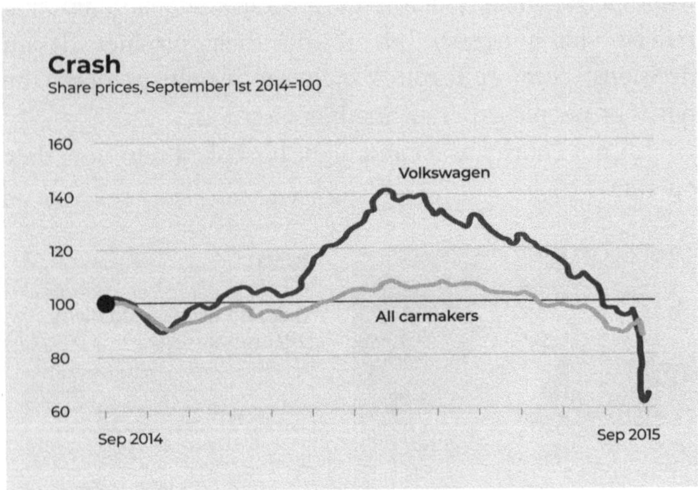

FIGURE 13: After Volkswagen's emission scandal was uncovered, its stocks plummeted and its CEO was deemed untenable

That's a textbook violation of congruence. And it cost them dearly: billions in fines, a crushed reputation, and lost trust that's still recovering. And while Volkswagen has made some progress in repairing their reputation and has made significant moves in becoming an authentic greener brand, this scandal will trigger skepticism among consumers for years to come.

Shein's Ethics vs. Advertising

Shein[10] markets itself as accessible, trend-forward, and even sustainable. They even have an institutionalized sustainability initiative called evoluShein.

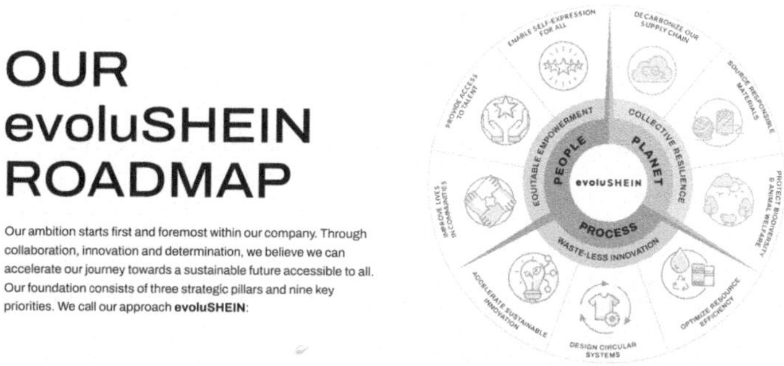

FIGURE 14: With the growing clamor for brands to be more environmentally-conscious, Shein spotlights its sustainability initiatives. However, people question the brand's authenticity as numerous reports reveal Shein's alleged impact to environmental degradation

But investigative reports continue to uncover labor violations, poor working conditions, and environmental harm[11].

They've tried influencer campaigns, charity partnerships, and greenwashing, but none of it sticks. Why? Because the brand's actions contradict its words.

Consumers can smell the disconnect.

HOW TO AUDIT YOUR BRAND FOR AUTHENTICITY

Here's a quick self-check you can use to assess how your brand measures up:

- Do you know (and document) what your brand stands for, and against?

- Does your tone of voice show up consistently across every channel?
- Are your internal values visible in external behaviors?
- If someone followed your brand for 30 days, would they walk away with a clear sense of who you are?

If the answer to any of those is fuzzy, it's time to tighten up.

YOU CAN'T FAKE THE FUNDAMENTALS

Authenticity isn't a soft skill. It's a structural advantage.

When you build a brand with clarity, consistency, and congruence, you're not just being "real." You're becoming recognizable. Trustworthy. Unmistakable.

You're building something people believe.

And in a world where everyone is selling something, belief is the most valuable asset you can earn.

CHAPTER 3
THE PSYCHOLOGY OF TRUST
WHY THE HUMAN BRAIN REWARDS HONEST MARKETING

Let's rewind for a moment. Before the brand strategy decks, before the marketing frameworks, before "authenticity" became a business buzzword, this idea started somewhere deeper. Somewhere older.

It started in the brain.

Because long before we were customers or clients, we were people. And people are wired to respond to authenticity.

Not because it's trendy.

But because it's trustworthy.

THE BRAIN ON AUTHENTICITY

When you encounter something that feels genuine, whether it's a brand, a person, or even a moment, your brain goes to work.

Studies in neuroscience[1] show that when people perceive honesty or congruence, it activates the prefrontal cortex, the part of the brain responsible for decision-making and trust evaluation[2].

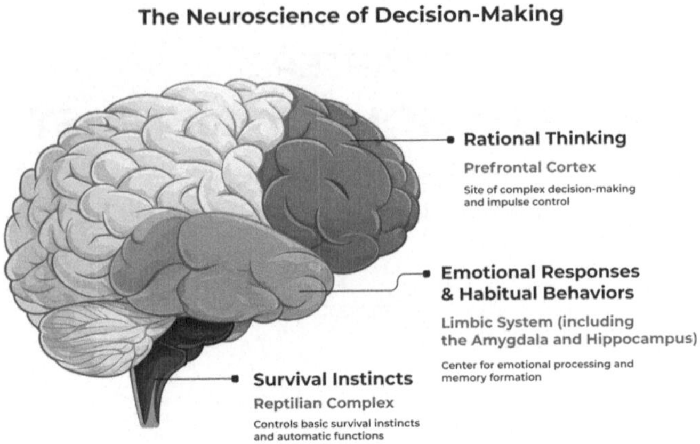

FIGURE 15: Authenticity taps into the brain's prefrontal complex which is responsible for decision-making

This isn't a metaphor. It's measurable.

When we sense a disconnect, like a brand saying one thing and doing another, that same area lights up, but in a different way, signaling risk.

Put simply:
Authenticity = psychological safety.

And psychological safety is the precursor to loyalty, to advocacy, to buying behavior.

This is why people rally around brands that stand for something. It's not just shared values, it's shared reality. It feels honest. It feels human. And that matters.

Why Trust Is a "Shortcut"

The human brain is lazy. Not in a bad way, just in an efficient way.

We're constantly filtering out noise to survive the overload of information around us. One of the filters we rely on? Trust.

Trust helps us make quick decisions without needing to evaluate every single variable. It's a cognitive shortcut, a way to say, "I've seen enough. I believe this."

That's why being genuine works better than trying to look perfect. Especially because trust has a direct impact on a business' bottomline.

We will discuss this further in a later chapter, but to give you an idea, according to the Edelman study[3], 59% of consumers are more likely to buy from a brand that they trust, even if their products are not as cheap and they are also more likely to buy their new products.

Additionally, when consumers trust a brand, they are 67% more likely to stay loyal to the business and recommend it to others:

Trust is earned through congruence. This happens when brands consistently follow through on what they promise.

THE ZEIGARNIK EFFECT AND INCONGRUENT BRANDS

Psychologist Bluma Zeigarnik discovered something fascinating: humans remember incomplete or interrupted tasks more than completed ones. It's called the Zeigarnik Effect.

This applies to brand behavior too.

When a brand starts a story, say, "We care deeply about the environment", but doesn't follow through with congruent action, our brains hold onto that disconnect. It creates cognitive tension. We're bothered. We don't forget.

And in today's world, when every consumer has a platform, that tension spreads.

Think of greenwashing. Or performative activism. When the words don't match the deeds, people remember, and share.

MIRROR NEURONS AND EMPATHY IN BRANDING

Another psychological force at play? Mirror neurons[4].

These are brain cells that fire both when we perform an action and when we observe someone else doing it. They're the reason we wince when someone stubs their toe, or cry during movie trailers.

When brands share stories or values that reflect our own beliefs, those mirror neurons kick in. We feel something. And feeling something is the precursor to remembering something.

This is why brands like Bombas, who build their mission into every product, create not just customers but believers. It's not just socks. It's a shared purpose. Shared emotion.

That emotional resonance is what makes authenticity stick.

THE PRINCIPLE OF CONGRUENCE (AND WHY IT MATTERS MORE THAN EVER)

In psychology, congruence refers to alignment between our ideal self and our actual self.

When we're around people, or brands, that display that

alignment, we subconsciously trust them more. It feels safe. Familiar. Right.

This matters even more in a marketing environment where consumers are trained to be skeptical.

Everyone's been burned by fake reviews, tone-deaf campaigns, bait-and-switch tactics. So we scan for clues:

- Does this brand say the same thing in email as it does in its ads?
- Do their values show up in their supply chain, not just their slogans?
- Do they talk to their customers like humans, or like a template?

When the answers are yes, yes, and yes, we lower our defenses. We let them in.

This isn't about being perfect. It's about being congruent.

And congruent brands are believable brands.

TALE OF CHOBANI YOGURT: VALUES IN ACTION

Let's bring this to life with a real-world example.

When Chobani[5] first hit shelves, it was just another Greek yogurt brand. But as it grew, it leaned hard into a simple but powerful idea: food should be made with natural ingredients, by a company that treats people well.

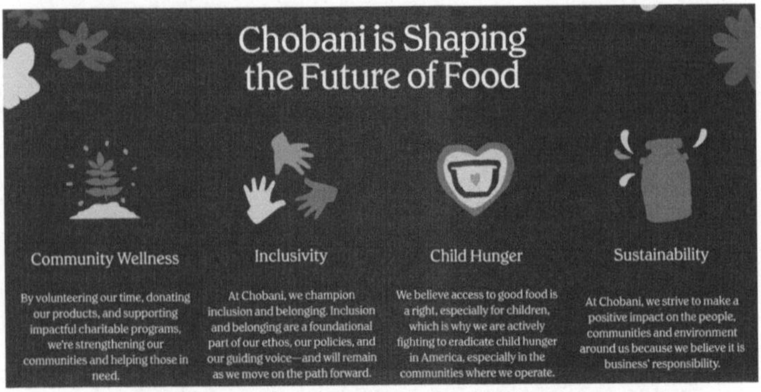

FIGURE 16: Chobani's advocacies are not only lip service or just to look good to sell their products. They're an integral part of who they are as a brand

And they backed it up:

- Paid above minimum wage to all factory workers
- Offered stock to all full-time employees
- Donated a portion of profits to support underserved communities
- Advocated for refugee hiring in manufacturing

This wasn't just a marketing gimmick, it was business policy.

As a result, Chobani didn't just build a brand. It built a community of loyal buyers who believed in the mission.

In an interview[6], Chobani Founder and CEO Hamdi Ulukaya said:

> *"It's very clear that the sole purpose of business is not just to make money for shareholders, but actually to look after their employees, their communities and their society. Businesses play a role in society, and they have a voice which they have to use. Silence is not an option. Businesses have an obligation to make sure their products*

and services meet the needs of humanity in a way that is not damaging, but healthy. These are the kinds of practices that you must have in business every single day, every single moment, it's much more important than ticking the box with CSR.

If businesses truly did everything – within the law – to make money for shareholders and nothing else, every single minute; it would mean destruction of capital in the medium to long term, and a company that is less innovative, less profitable, and slower. We need broader perspectives, and an understanding that shareholders are not the only stakeholders. You have to serve all your stakeholders to ensure they are all lifted. That makes you fast, innovative and profitable and these kinds of values do not go against business, they are intrinsically a part of it".

Their success wasn't just about good yogurt. It was about believable values.

BURGER KING'S "REAL MEALS" MISSTEP: A CASE STUDY IN INCONGRUENCE

In 2019, Burger King launched *Real Meals* as a counterpoint to McDonald's Happy Meals. The campaign[7] was themed around mental health, with meal names like "Pissed Meal" and "Blue Meal," accompanied by the slogan: "No one is happy all the time."

FIGURE 17: While well-meaning, Burger King's Real Meal campaign faced backlash due to the oversimplification of mental health issues and zero track record of supporting mental health causes

The idea? Normalize mental health struggles.

The issue? Burger King had no prior history of supporting mental health initiatives, and critics quickly pointed out that their own workplace practices didn't reflect this messaging.

Without meaningful action to back it up, the campaign felt opportunistic. Like Pepsi's ad, it was perceived as performative, not authentic.

The backlash wasn't just about taste. It was about trust.

WHY WE'RE SKEPTICAL OF BRANDS IN THE FIRST PLACE

There's a reason brands have to work harder today than ever before to earn trust.

We've seen behind the curtain.

We've watched documentaries about sweatshops.

We've read exposes about fast fashion.

We've seen influencers stage fake vacations.

We've lived through ad tracking scandals and data breaches.

We're trained to be suspicious.

So when a brand shows up with clean design and clever copy, that's not enough anymore. We want proof. We want alignment. We want the receipts.

Authenticity, in this context, becomes a trust accelerant. It tells our skeptical brains: This brand might actually mean it.

THE FAMILIARITY PRINCIPLE: REPETITION BREEDS BELIEF

Here's another psychological principle in play: the mere-exposure effect[8].

Also called the familiarity principle, it says that the more we're exposed to something, the more we tend to like it, as long as it feels consistent and safe.

This is where consistency (one of the 3 Cs) becomes so powerful. When your brand shows up in the same tone, with the same values, across multiple platforms, people don't just recognize you, they begin to believe you.

The exposure turns into trust. The trust turns into action.

But the opposite is also true: when your voice shifts wildly from email to social to site, it creates cognitive friction. That friction slows trust. Or kills it altogether.

RECAPPING THE PSYCHOLOGY OF TRUST

When you understand the psychology behind authenticity, you stop treating it like a vibe, and start treating it like a strategy.

Because:

- Authenticity creates psychological safety
- Congruence builds trust
- Trust accelerates decision-making
- Emotional alignment drives loyalty

This isn't marketing fluff. It's human nature.

The brands that win don't just have good ideas. They have believable ones.

And in the next chapter, we'll talk about how to translate that believability into writing that people actually want to read.

CHAPTER 4
HOW TO MAKE YOUR BRAND MORE AUTHENTIC
PRACTICAL WAYS TO BE REAL, WITHOUT LOSING SALES

Let's talk about execution. Because authenticity isn't just a mindset, it's a muscle. It's something you train, refine, and apply across every layer of your brand.

But here are the challenges:

- How do you sound real, without sounding amateur?
- How do you market effectively without over hyping?
- How do you sell without sounding like you're selling?

This chapter gives you the tools to answer all of that.

Not abstract theory, practical tactics.

Because authenticity doesn't have to be a trade-off. You can drive conversions and build trust at the same time.

Let's dig in.

AUDIT YOUR BRAND VOICE, MESSAGING, AND VISUALS

Before you change what you say, take a long, honest look at what you're currently putting out there.

Start with a simple audit:

- Is your tone human or templated?
- Does your messaging reflect your customer's real-life situation, or your product's ideal use case?
- Are your visuals consistent, intentional, and reflective of your values?

Here's where many brands go wrong:

- They outsource tone to ChatGPT prompts.
- They pattern a landing page from ten competitors.
- They let visuals be dictated by trends instead of truth.

You can't fake congruence. So go through your:

- Homepage
- Social media captions
- Product pages
- Email nurture flows

And ask: Does this feel like a real person made it for another real person?

If the answer's no, don't panic. We're about to walk through how to fix it.

ALIGN YOUR OFFER WITH YOUR AUDIENCE'S REAL PROBLEM

Most marketing gets ignored not because the offer is bad, but because it's solving the wrong problem.

Real authenticity starts with real relevance.

If you sell a time-tracking app:

What You Think You're Selling	What You're Actually Selling
Better Time Tracking	Less chaos at work Fewer missed tasks A team that hits deadlines without burnout

If you sell financial coaching:

What You Think You're Selling	What You're Actually Selling
Better Spreadsheets	The confidence to quit that toxic job The peace of mind to stop checking your bank account 3X a day

This is where authenticity meets empathy.

Your message should meet your audience where they actually are, not where your product roadmap says they should be.

Authentic storytelling happens in the "sweet spot", the overlap between what your brand truly believes and what your audience actually cares about. If your message leans only on your brand's priorities, it feels self-serving. If it leans only on the audience without reflecting your values, it feels hollow. The real magic happens when both overlap: your internal beliefs and external actions align with your audience's beliefs and behaviors.

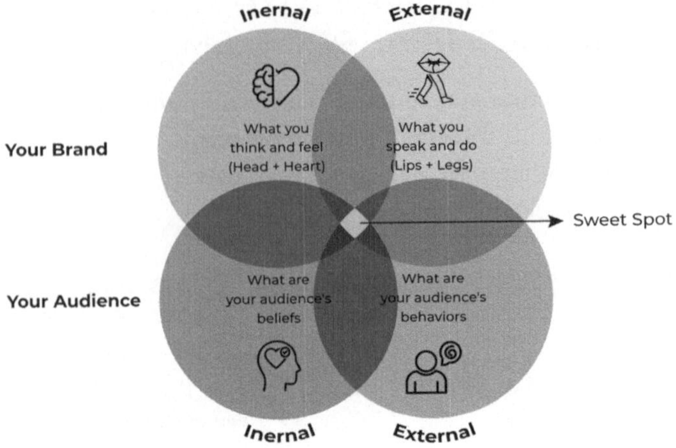

FIGURE 18: The "sweet spot" of authenticity sits where your brand's voice meets your audience's values and behaviors, the zone where stories resonate and drive trust.

Ask yourself:

- What's frustrating them at 8am?
- What's keeping them up at 11pm?
- What's the real, human problem they'd pay to fix?

Then build your message around that, not features or hype.

CUT THE HYPE, KEEP THE CLARITY

Here's a hard truth: Most marketing copy sounds like marketing copy.

It's full of empty superlatives:

- World-class customer support!

- Industry-leading innovation!
- The best solution for modern businesses!

None of it means anything.

People don't believe what you say about yourself.

They believe what they can see, feel, or verify.

So instead of saying you're fast, show a real customer who got their results in three days.

Instead of claiming "unparalleled design", show a GIF walkthrough or real feedback from your users.

Remember: Clarity is more persuasive than hype.

Because clarity builds trust. And trust converts.

Here's a before/after to drive it home:

BEFORE	AFTER
"Our game-changing software will revolutionize your business."	"Our platform helped 4,300 small businesses cut admin work by 22%, without adding headcount."

One is forgettable. The other is believable.

USE TESTIMONIALS, FOUNDER STORIES, BEHIND-THE-SCENES CONTENT

People don't connect with logos. They connect with other people.

That's why testimonials, founder stories, and BTS content are some of the most effective (and underused) tools in building an authentic brand.

Let's break them down:

Testimonials

Not just praise, but specific praise.

"Their team changed the way we communicate" is okay.

"Their onboarding playbook helped our 9-person team cut client churn in half in 60 days" is better.

Use screenshots, video clips, actual names and faces when possible. Social proof should look and sound like it came from real customers, because it did.

Founder Stories

People love to know why you built what you built.

Was it out of frustration? Obsession? Necessity?

Don't be afraid to share the origin story, even if it's messy or imperfect. It humanizes your brand and creates emotional stakes.

Let's go back to the example of Chobani CEO Hamdi Ulukaya. In another interview with Adi Ignatius[1] of Harvard Business Review, he said:

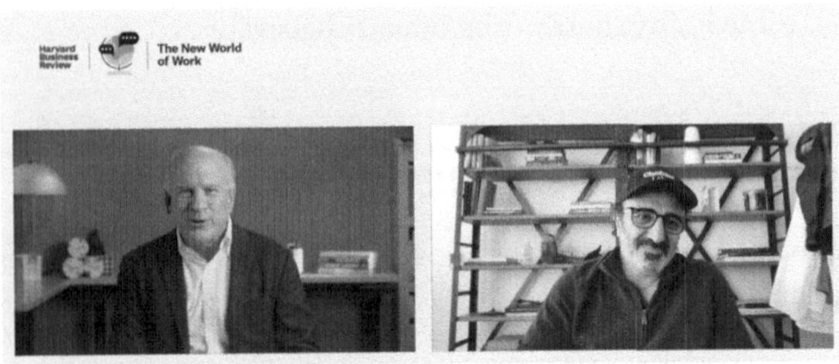

FIGURE 19: Chobani CEO Hamdi Ulukaya in conversation with Harvard Business Review's Adi Ignatius, discussing his roots, values, and the importance of staying connected to the communities that brands serve

"Especially in our field, I come from, like you said, a rural part of Turkey. I don't come from rich or well-off type of areas. We come

from the villagers and factory workers, working class, and there's a disconnect. Of course, this struggle has been all around the world, but there's a disconnect when it comes to wealth, when it comes to access to even state resources and you come to upstate New York and you see the same thing. The factory gets closed, the company make a decision in, I don't know, whatever, Chicago in a tower, and the community is left behind and workers are to blame. Now this is the same thing going on when it comes to manufacturing, when it comes to rural areas of the work and environment that is controlled by the large corporations, this injustice is in a level of affecting people's life in a very, very dramatic way.

When it comes to starting Chobani in that old factory, I always wanted to say, "Can I start a company? Can I start Chobani, not to follow the footsteps of the company that closed it?"

The second angle is, when I grow up and I said I never liked the ones that are greedy or the rich or whatever you call it, how do I build a place where I don't become a person that I grew up hating? That was the blueprint. In that, four factory workers and myself, we started this place. My first promise I made is the people who will build this company with me will always be center of this place and always be recognized in all dimension, including financially. And can I make an example, that the people that left behind, people that were forgotten, especially in food making and manufacturing, how do I make them the most important people in the company?"

Being allowed to be let into that light bulb moment when a brand is born builds a strong emotional connection with its ideal audience.

Behind-the-Scenes (BTS) Content

Show your process. Your people. Your values in action.
What does product testing actually look like?
What's on your whiteboard right now?

What debates happen in your team meetings?

BTS doesn't have to be fancy, it just has to be real.

When people see your work behind the curtain, they're more likely to trust what's on the main stage.

This is easy if you have nothing to hide. It doesn't mean that you have to be perfect. It just means that you can take accountability of everything that goes on behind the scenes.

AVOID MANIPULATION TACTICS THAT ERODE TRUST

There's a line between urgency and manipulation.

Between persuasion and pressure.

If you cross that line, you break trust.

Here's what to watch out for:

Fake countdown timers: If the offer never really expires, don't pretend it does.

1. **Shady anchor pricing:** Listing $499 as the "original" price when it never sold for more than $199 is dishonest.
2. **Over-personalized AI emails:** Just because you scraped someone's first name doesn't mean you've earned their attention.
3. **Artificial scarcity:** "Only 2 seats left" when that's not true. These tactics may temporarily boost conversions, but it destroys long-term trust.

Instead, focus on:

- Real deadlines
- Clear benefits

- Transparent pricing
- Honest testimonials

You don't need to manipulate to convert. You just need to resonate.

10 WAYS TO MAKE YOUR MARKETING MORE BELIEVABLE

Let's wrap with a tactical checklist you can use today:

- Replace vague claims with specifics
- Use testimonials with results, not fluff
- Tell your origin story
- Audit for tone
- Show the real people behind the brand
- Ditch manipulative urgency
- Avoid perfection
- Share your "why" regularly
- Make your values visible in your supply chain, your pricing, your policies
- Stay consistent across every channel

AUTHENTICITY IS A COMPETITIVE ADVANTAGE, IF YOU COMMIT TO IT

Most brands will never do this work.

They'll keep chasing the latest tactic.

They'll keep polishing fake urgency.

They'll keep hiding behind jargon and automation.

But not you.

If you choose clarity over hype, empathy over manipulation, real connection over conversion gimmicks...

You won't just make your brand feel more authentic.

You'll make it more profitable.

Because trust is the new moat.

And the brands who earn it will keep winning.

Next up: How to write like a real human being, even when you're trying to sell.

CHAPTER 5

AUTHENTIC FUNNELS THAT CONVERT

EMAILS, ADS, AND PAGES PEOPLE TRUST

It's one thing to say your brand is authentic. It's another to make every part of your marketing funnel reflect that.

The truth is, most customers don't experience your mission statement or your values doc. They experience your ads. Your emails. Your landing pages.

That's where authenticity has to show up, or it doesn't count.

In this chapter, we'll break down how to build trust into every step of your marketing system. With copy that sounds like a real person. Ads that convert because they're clear, not clever. And emails that respect people's time and attention.

We'll also look at brands that are actually doing this right, so you're not left guessing.

WRITE LIKE A PERSON, NOT A PITCH DECK

Marketing today suffers from what we can call "corporate karaoke." Everyone's singing the same tune. Buzzwords. Boilerplate. Brand-safe fluff.

Real copy breaks through the noise because it sounds like a human being.

How to spot inauthentic copy	How to write authentically
Leads with jargon: "Scalable cloud-based solutions..."	Use contractions, short sentences, and natural phrasing
Uses empty modifiers: "world-class," "innovative," "best-in-class"	Show emotion and opinion: "Honestly, we were tired of wasting money on tools that didn't work."
Avoids specifics: "trusted by hundreds" (but shows no proof)	Be clear, not clever: "We help freelancers send invoices faster."

One great rule of thumb: Would you actually say this sentence in a conversation with a friend? If not, rewrite it.

AUTHENTIC ADS THAT ACTUALLY CONVERT

Most Facebook and Instagram ads try too hard. The result? They blend into a sea of sameness.

But the best-performing authentic ads share some common traits:

Trait	Bad	Better
They're specific, not sensational.	"Transform your life with our breakthrough system!"	"Tired of forgetting what you read? This app helps you remember books with 5-minute summaries."
They feel native to the platform	A polished graphic with all caps and buzzwords.	A selfie-style video from the founder explaining how they built the product.
They speak to the reader, not at them.	"Our customers love our intuitive interface."	"You won't need a manual. If you can send an email, you can use this."

Kinfield[1], a clean skincare brand, uses Instagram ads that feel like recommendations from a friend, not commercials. Their creative often features:

- Founders talking on camera
- Real customer clips
- Clear problem-solution headlines ("Mosquito spray that actually works.")

FIGURE 20: Kinfield leverages the power of user generated content to promote their products in a more organic way

They don't try to impress, they try to connect.

EMAIL SEQUENCES THAT BUILD TRUST (NOT RESENTMENT)

Most email sequences feel like digital nagging.

They scream urgency, beg for clicks, and often skip the trust-building phase altogether.

Here's how to stand out:

1. Lead with value, not pitch.

- Share a surprising stat
- Offer a tip that solves a small but painful problem
- Ask a question that sparks thought

2. Be radically clear about what's next.

- "In tomorrow's email, I'll show you how to do [X] without [painful Y]."

3. Make it personal (not creepy).

- Use your real name and face
- Write in first-person
- Don't fake personalization, earn attention through usefulness

Everyday Dose, a mushroom-based coffee alternative, sends a welcome email that:

- Features a letter from the founder
- Shares the "why" behind the brand
- Links to a behind-the-scenes video on how the product is made

EVERYDAY DOSE

Hi there! I'm Jack, founder of Everyday Dose.

So happy you're here. As promised, here's your 40% OFF and free gifts!

Why Everyday Dose?

We created a revolutionary coffee blend that fuels your mind and body, helping you feel a little bit better, every day. It's coffee, plus benefits.

We combine powerful ingredients like:

- Lion's Mane (for brain power)
- Chaga (an antioxidant powerhouse)
- Collagen Protein (for healthy joints, hair, and nails)
- L-Theanine (to reduce stress and improve focus)
- Coffee Extract (for a smooth, low-acidity caffeine boost)

Over 300,000 happy customers have already upgraded their coffee routine with Everyday Dose, experiencing sustained focus and energy.

Ready to Experience the Difference?

Claim Your 40% OFF + FREE Starter Kit Here! It's time to transform your daily energy and focus!

You Got This,

Jack
Founder of Everyday Dose

P.S. Curious about the full story behind Everyday Dose? Read my journey here!

Shop About

EVERYDAY DOSE™

ON A MISSION TO MAKE COFFEE HEALTHIER.

*These statements have not been evaluated by the Food and Drug Administration. This product is not intended to diagnose, treat, cure or prevent any disease.

© Everyday Dose Inc, 2025. All Rights Reserved.

FIGURE 21: Every Dose's welcome email may not be fancy in terms of design, but its authenticity provides a good start for customers to connect with the brand.

It feels like a handshake, not a sale.

LANDING PAGES THAT CONVERT BECAUSE THEY'RE REAL

Here's a brutal truth: Most landing pages are lying.

They overpromise. They under-explain. And they're terrified of being boring, so they compensate with flash.

Authentic landing pages convert because they're honest.

1. Make the headline sound like your customer

- Instead of: "Revolutionary Time Management Platform for Agile Teams"
- Try: "Your team's drowning in deadlines. We help you stay ahead"

2. Show real humans

Stock photos kill trust. Use:

- Actual user photos
- Behind-the-scenes shots
- Lo-fi product walkthroughs

3. Use real testimonials, and don't hide them

- Place testimonials on a noticeable section on the page
- Make them specific
- Attribute them properly

Goodr[2], a sunglasses brand, uses a product page layout that:

- Leads with on-brand product description
- Includes photos from real customers on Instagram
- Easy to understand product features and benefits presented in simple visuals

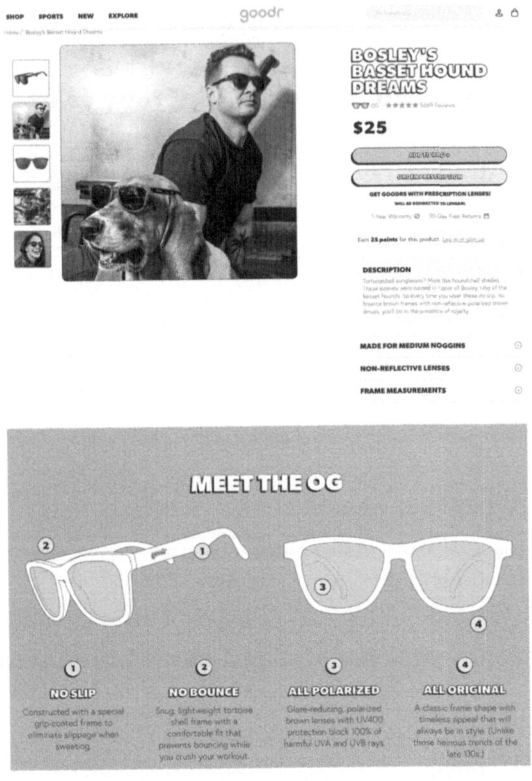

FIGURE 22: Authenticity in product pages like that of Goodr builds trust and connection with customers at the point of purchase

TEARDOWN: FAKE FUNNEL VS. AUTHENTIC FUNNEL

Let's compare two versions of a funnel for a fictional product: a digital planner app.

"FAKE" FUNNEL	AUTHENTIC FUNNEL
AD "This #1-rated productivity hack will 10x your output instantly!" (stock image + fake countdown timer)	**AD** "We built this because Google Docs wasn't cutting it. Here's what we made." (founder on video)
LANDING PAGE Vague headline, no pricing, hidden reviews	**LANDING PAGE** Clear pain point ("Still forgetting things? Let's fix that."), transparent pricing, reviews with photos
EMAILS 5-day hard-sell sequence with fake urgency ("Only 3 seats left!")	**EMAILS** 5-day sequence walking through product use, sharing team notes, offering value before asking for the sale

BRANDS GETTING THIS RIGHT (AND WHAT YOU CAN LEARN FROM THEM)

Let's spotlight a few brands that actually execute what we've covered:

1. Blume

- Personal care brand[3] targeting Gen Z.
- Their ads feature real acne journeys and before/afters.
- Their emails are funny, honest, and founder-led.

- Their product pages use relatable headlines like: "Zits suck. Let's deal with them."

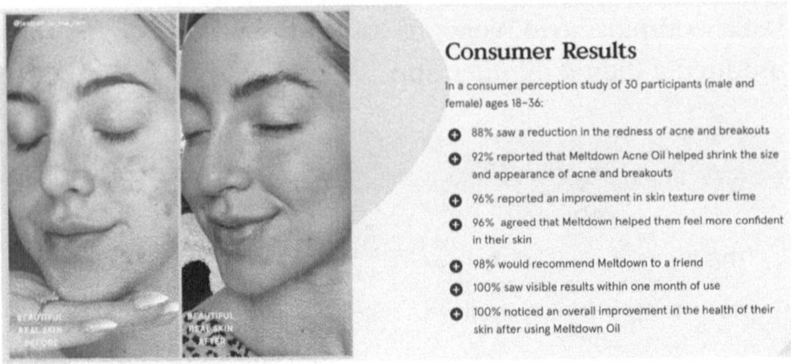

FIGURE 23: Specificity builds authenticity and customer confidence

2. Bark Box

- Keeps a humorous tone from its social media posts, to its website[4], to its emails.
- Uses a playful voice that reflects real life scenarios when fur parents talk to their fur babies.
- Keep the same tone even in internal operations (for example, phone representatives are called "Phone Pups").

FIGURE 24: The ability to mirror your customers' voice is a positive sign of authentic marketing

3. Dove

- It's Real Beauty campaign[5], now called Self Esteem Project, has withstood the test of time since being launched in 2004.
- The messages have been consistent in redefining beauty.
- Often featured real women and did not hide their insecurities about their appearance.

FIGURE 25: Dove's Real Beauty Sketches video garnered 50 million views a mere 12 days. According to Dove's website, it has now gained 180 million views overall since it was launched in 2013

What These Brands Have in Common:

- Specificity over superlatives
- Real faces over stock images
- Transparency over trickery
- Story over spin

They've figured out what works: Not louder marketing, but more honest marketing.

And they prove you don't have to choose between sales and sincerity.

IF IT FEELS REAL, IT CONVERTS BETTER

The irony of modern marketing is that the less you try to sell, the more you often do sell.

Because authenticity builds trust. And trust compounds.

So whether you're writing an ad, building an email sequence, or redesigning your landing page, ask yourself:

"Does this sound like something a real person would actually say?"

If not, change it.

In the next chapter, we'll go deeper into storytelling: how to craft origin stories and founder narratives that make people root for your brand (and hit that Buy button).

Because behind every real brand is a real story worth telling.

CHAPTER 6

KEEPING IT REAL IN THE AGE OF AI

USING AUTOMATION WITHOUT LOSING YOUR VOICE

Let's not dance around it:

AI is here, and it's not going anywhere.

A SmartInsights survey[1] revealed that 40% of businesses are using ChatGPT to improve marketing performance.

For entrepreneurs, small businesses, and lean marketing teams, it can feel like the cavalry has finally arrived.

You can generate content faster. You can automate tasks that used to eat hours. You can keep up with bigger competitors who have entire departments for what you do between Zoom calls.

But with all that power comes a new kind of pressure: How do you keep your brand real when machines are doing the talking?

The truth is, authenticity isn't about who writes your content. It's about the intention behind it, the clarity of your voice, and your commitment to showing up as you.

WHY AI IS INEVITABLE (AND THAT'S NOT A BAD THING)

If you're a solopreneur or part of a small team, you're not choosing between using AI or not. You're choosing between:

- Getting stuff done and reaching people
- Burning out trying to do everything manually

AI isn't a shortcut. It's a tool. It's like hiring a really fast assistant who can give you 20 drafts in 20 seconds. According to HubSpot's 2025 AI Trends for Marketers[2], 84% agree that AI helped them produce content more efficiently.

But you're still the creative director. You still decide what's on-brand. You still make the calls.

The brands that win in the age of AI won't be the ones that resist it. They'll be the ones that use it thoughtfully.

THE RISK: LOSING THE HUMAN TOUCH

We've all seen what happens when brands lean too hard on AI:

- Every Instagram caption sounds like it was written by a chatbot
- Emails are technically correct but emotionally vacant
- Websites feel like content farms in disguise

If you use AI without human oversight, you'll end up sounding like everyone else using AI without human oversight.

That's the real risk: not the tool, but *the temptation to stop thinking*.

Authenticity isn't just about having a human write the words. It's about:

- Having a recognizable tone
- Telling honest stories
- Being consistent with your values
- Speaking directly to your audience's real problems

None of that gets outsourced.

WHAT "AUTHENTIC AI MARKETING" ACTUALLY LOOKS LIKE

Let's make this concrete.

Authentic AI marketing means using AI to:

- Speed up the boring stuff (e.g., generating outlines, transcribing interviews, writing first drafts)
- Free yourself up to do the meaningful stuff (e.g., shaping the message, adding personality, making final decisions)
- Sound more like yourself, not less

In practice, that could look like:

- Asking AI to write a rough draft of your blog post, then rewriting it in your voice
- Using AI to summarize a customer interview, then pulling real quotes to include in your copy

- Getting headline suggestions and using your gut to pick the one that feels most "you"

You don't have to fake a personality. You just have to show up. AI helps you get there faster.

A FRAMEWORK: REALNESS AT EVERY STEP

Here's a simple framework for keeping your marketing authentic, even when AI is involved:

1. Be Clear on Your Voice

Define it. Are you playful? Authoritative? Casual? Weird? Whatever it is, make it consistent.

Save examples of your past writing you love and use them as benchmarks.

2. Use AI for the First 80%, Not the Last 20%

AI is great for scaffolding. But the magic happens in the edit.

Use tools like ChatGPT, Claude, Jasper, etc., to get started, but never publish without a human pass.

3. Always Fact-Check and Gut-Check

AI can be confident and wrong at the same time. According to HubSpot[3], 43% of users report inaccurate information generated by AI platforms.

Don't outsource judgment.

If something doesn't feel like you, it probably isn't.

4. Leave Room for Humanity

Add personal stories. Reference real experiences. Use first names.

These touches are what make content feel lived-in and alive.

5. Test and Listen

If something flops, it's not the tool's fault. It's a signal.

Keep listening to your audience. They'll tell you when you've veered off course.

THE MYTH OF "FULLY AUTHENTIC, FULLY HUMAN"

Some purists argue that real authenticity means no AI involvement. That's a nice idea, but let's be real.

Most of your audience:

- Doesn't care if you used AI
- Can't tell if you used AI
- Just wants content that helps, entertains, or inspires them

Your job isn't to avoid AI.

Your job is to keep the soul of your message alive.

That might mean writing every word yourself. Or it might mean using a robot to rough it out so you can focus on the magic parts.

Either way, authenticity comes from you.

WHEN TO NOT USE AI

There are some places where AI just doesn't belong, or at least needs extra scrutiny:

- Sensitive responses (like customer support for an angry customer)
- Controversial topics (where nuance and tone really matter)
- Highly technical or legal content (where incorrect info = big problems)
- Anything where your gut says: "This has to be me"

If it's personal, emotional, or reputation-critical, write it yourself. Or at the very least, edit it like your name's going on it. Because it is.

HOW TO TRAIN AI TO SOUND LIKE YOU

Want to go deeper? You can actually train AI tools to sound more like you:

- **Feed it your past writing:** Give it examples of emails, posts, captions, etc.
- **Explain your quirks:** Do you use contractions? Pop culture refs? Emojis? Dry humor?
- **Give it feedback:** Tell it what you like and don't like. It learns.

Over time, you can build a custom voice model that mirrors your style. That doesn't make it you, but it gets a lot closer than a blank prompt.

AT THE END OF THE DAY, YOU ARE NOT REPLACEABLE

The fear many marketers and creatives have is: "Will I still be needed if AI gets better?"

Here's the honest truth: If your only skill is typing words, maybe not. But if your skill is thinking, connecting, seeing what others miss, and speaking human?

You're irreplaceable.

The best marketers of the AI age will use AI. But they won't become it.

They'll stand out because their content feels like someone real made it.

And in a world of generated everything, real is what converts.

CHAPTER 7
THE ROI OF BEING REAL
HOW AUTHENTICITY DRIVES GROWTH AND PROFIT

Let's start with a green owl.

When Duolingo[1], the language-learning app, launched its TikTok strategy, no one expected it to become a case study in brand voice. But it did, by being completely, unapologetically real.

Instead of pushing polished promos or influencer partnerships, Duolingo unleashed its mascot, Duo, in a chaotic flurry of unhinged humor. He twerked in the office. He thirsted after Dua Lipa. He roasted users who skipped lessons. It was bizarre. Off-brand, some said.

And yet, it was brilliant.

Within months, Duolingo had racked up millions of followers, viral videos, and a cultural moment most brands would kill for. All by ditching the "brand safe" route and embracing something rare in marketing: authenticity.

For example, in a more recent video, as of the writing of this book, Duolingo posted this funny video of its app's characters[2] seemingly unconscious with crosses on their eyes. The caption reads: "We believe in transparency and wanted to share this heartbreaking update. We are investigating and will keep all informed. #RipDuo #RipEveryone.

FIGURE 26: Duolingo's TikTok posts exemplify that non-corporate, non-sterile marketing messages can work as long as they remain faithful to a brand's identity

This was followed by a post by Duolingo CEO Luis von Ahn "paying tribute[3]" to Duo, saying: "In his honor, let's do what he would have wanted. Open up the app, do a lesson, and share your fondest memories."

FIGURE 27:Duolingo CEO Luis von Ahn "paying tribute"

As of this writing, the two posts have garnered more than 17 million views, 1.2 million likes, and 30,000 comments in total.

More than the likes and the engagement, the most important are the conversions.

Downloads spiked.

Revenue climbed.

Duolingo didn't just entertain; they earned.

Their voice wasn't slick. It was specific. Honest. Human.

And in today's market, that's the difference between being remembered, or ignored.

WHY AUTHENTICITY PAYS

There's a myth in marketing that being "authentic" is soft. That it's about feelings, fluff, and tone. That it's nice to have, but not necessary if you've got a strong offer, killer creative, and a high enough ad budget.

Wrong.

Authenticity isn't just good vibes, it drives revenue. Loyalty. Lifetime value. Word of mouth. In a digital world where trust is the scarcest commodity, being real is one of the most profitable moves a brand can make.

Let's break down exactly why, and show you what it looks like when brands bet on realness (and win).

REAL-WORLD EXAMPLE: PATAGONIA'S PURPOSE-LED PROFIT

Patagonia is a masterclass in authentic branding.

The outdoor gear company doesn't just market its values, it lives them. From donating 1% of all sales to environmental causes, to suing the government over protected land rollbacks, to literally running an ad[4] that said "Don't Buy This Jacket" to discourage overconsumption, Patagonia walks its talk.

FIGURE 28: In 2011, Patagonia released an advertisement in the New York Times to discourage customers from buying their jackets and avoid overconsumption. This is a bold move for a clothing brand, especially because the ad was released on a Black Friday, America's peak shopping season

However, it's not all gimmick. In an article published on its website, Patagonia said:

> *"It would be hypocritical for us to work for environmental change without encouraging customers to think before they buy. To reduce environmental damage, we all have to reduce consumption as well as make products in more environmentally sensitive, less harmful ways. It's not hypocrisy for us to address the need to reduce consumption. On the other hand, it's folly to assume that a healthy economy can be based on buying and selling more and more things people don't need—and it's time for people who believe that's folly to say so.*
>
> *Nevertheless, Patagonia is a growing business—and we want to be in business a good long time. The test of our sincerity (or our hypocrisy) will be if everything we sell is useful, multifunctional where possible, long lasting, beautiful but not in thrall to fashion. We're not yet entirely there. Not every product meets all these criteria. Our Common Threads Initiative will serve as a framework to advance us toward these goals"*

In 2022, founder Yvon Chouinard went even further: he gave the entire company away. Not to his children. Not to a holding firm. But to a nonprofit trust designed to fight climate change.

Let that sink in: a billion-dollar business handed over in the name of values.

And the result? Patagonia continues to thrive. Their customer base is fiercely loyal. Their brand equity is off the charts. And while they may not chase growth like a VC-backed tech startup, they have something better: deep, durable trust.

They're not just selling jackets. They're selling belief, and people are buying.

SMALL BRANDS, BIG IMPACT: THE RISE OF HONEST ECOMMERCE

It's not just billion-dollar companies that benefit from authenticity. In fact, smaller brands often win because they can be more real.

Take Death Wish Coffee[5]. They built an entire business on being unapologetically bold, strongest coffee in the world, skull-and-crossbones branding, aggressive humor. Their brand voice doesn't appeal to everyone. But that's the point. It feels like someone, not "everyone." And that clarity drives loyalty.

FIGURE 29 Death wish coffee demonstrates authenticity with bold messages that stays true to who they are and what their tribe relates to

Or consider Brooklinen[6], the direct-to-consumer bedding company that took off by being radically transparent. They shared their supply chain details. They broke down manufacturing costs. Their tone? Casual, unfussy, and real. They didn't pretend to be a luxury brand. They leaned into being high-quality without the markup. That honesty resonated, helping them grow from a Kickstarter project to a $100M+ company.

FIGURE 30: From its inception, Brooklinen has practiced a high level of authenticity by allowing customers access to what happens behind the scenes

The takeaway? You don't need a giant budget. You need a human voice and the guts to stick to it.

AUTHENTICITY AS A CONVERSION STRATEGY

Let's be blunt: most people don't trust your marketing.

They've been burned too many times. Seen too many bait-and-switch offers. Read too many LinkedIn posts written by ChatGPT pretending to be a "vulnerable founder."

So when they do come across a brand that feels honest? That speaks clearly, with empathy, from experience?

It's magnetic.

Your landing pages don't need to scream. Your emails don't need to oversell. Because the trust has already been established.

And that trust lowers the cost of acquisition. It increases lifetime value. It accelerates word of mouth.

That's not fluff. That's the strategy

AUTHENTICITY MAKES MARKETING SUSTAINABLE

Most marketing tactics are extractive. Push harder. Spend more. Squeeze the list.

But authenticity? It builds equity over time. It makes your future campaigns easier, not harder. Because instead of renting attention, you're earning allegiance.

When you're real from day one:

- People remember your name
- They forgive your mistakes
- They root for your success
- They come back (even when cheaper alternatives exist)

That's brand insurance. That's real ROI.

WHAT YOU CAN START DOING RIGHT NOW

Want to cash in on the ROI of authenticity? Here's where to start:

1. Audit your brand voice

Does it sound like a person or a press release? Strip out the corporate lingo. Inject warmth, honesty, edge, whatever feels real for your brand.

2. Show the behind-the-scenes

Pull back the curtain. Show the people, process, and imperfections. Audiences connect with what feels human.

3. Highlight real customers

Share authentic testimonials and real use cases. When people see others benefiting from your product, it builds instant trust, because trust is contagious.

4. Lead with values

What does your brand stand for, and against? Don't hide it. Own it. Let people buy into more than just the product.

Say "we messed up" when you mess up. Accountability isn't weakness. It's credibility.

Tell the truth in your marketing. Not the spin. Not the sugarcoating. Just the truth. Say what your product actually does. And why you built it. That's what converts.

YOU CAN'T AFFORD TO BE FAKE

Here's the bottom line: people can smell a performance. They can sense a pitch. And they can feel when something is off.

But they can also feel when something is real. When a message lands. When a brand speaks their language. That moment of connection? That's where trust begins.

And once you have it?

You can build anything.

So don't be the brand that hides behind polish, jargon,

or cleverness. Be the one that earns trust, by showing up, being clear, and keeping it real.

Because authenticity doesn't just feel good. It pays.

BE REAL, OR BE FORGOTTEN

We've come full circle.

You've made it through the psychology, the principles, the checklists, the frameworks, the teardown examples, and the callouts to AI. But at the end of the day, the message of this book is not about copywriting.

It's about truth.

Because marketing doesn't need more tactics, it needs more truth.

In a world oversaturated with messages, offers, hooks, and headlines, the only thing that breaks through is what feels real. Not real-sounding. Not well-branded. Not tastefully vulnerable. Actually real.

And here's the plot twist:

The truth sells.

We've been told for decades that persuasion requires a bit of spin. That to move people, you need urgency, exclusivity, manufactured scarcity. You need "positioning." You need psychology hacks. You need neuro-linguistic programming.

But the truth, when it's specific, when it's relevant, when it's brave, is more powerful than all of that.

It's not just that consumers are savvier. It's not just that they've been burned before. It's not just that they're scrolling past your ad in milliseconds.

It's that we're all drowning in inauthenticity.

And when something cuts through with clarity, honesty, and specificity, it sticks.

RECAP: WHAT AUTHENTIC MARKETING REALLY MEANS

Let's bring it all together.

1. Authenticity isn't a vibe, it's a practice.

It's not about tone. It's about decisions. Real offers. Real language. Real values lived out loud.

2. Trust is the new conversion rate.

If someone trusts you, they'll open your emails, click your links, and even wait for your next product. If they don't, no amount of "funnels" will save you.

3. Specificity sells.

Don't say "great customer service." Say "we reply in under 2 hours, even on weekends." Don't say "our customers love us." Show the review that says, "This saved my launch when nothing else worked."

4. Be human.

Write like a person. Show your face. Share your journey. Own your weirdness. Speak the way you'd speak to someone you like, not someone you're trying to "convert."

5. You don't need to be perfect. You need to be clear.

Stop trying to sound bigger than you are. Say what you actually do. Say who it's really for. And say it in plain English.

Authentic marketing isn't soft. It's not naive. It's not some new-age, "brand with purpose" fluff.

It's one of the most powerful competitive advantages you have.

And it's available to every single business, especially the ones willing to be honest when everyone else is hiding behind buzzwords.

TRY THIS IN YOUR NEXT CAMPAIGN

Let's leave you with something simple. Something practical. Something you can actually do this week.

Run a marketing campaign with one goal: Earn trust, don't ask for anything.

Here's what that could look like:

- A 3-email welcome series that doesn't sell, just tells your story, shares useful tips, and explains why you built this in the first place.
- A landing page that strips away the hype and simply says: "Here's the problem. Here's our

solution. Here's how it works. Here's what others say."

- An ad that doesn't pitch, but teaches. That makes someone feel something. That offers a new perspective instead of a discount code.

- A social post that shares the biggest mistake you made in your business, and what it taught you.

You don't have to turn your brand into a memoir. You don't have to overshare. You just have to stop pretending, and start connecting.

Be clear.

Be honest.

Be a little less polished, a little more real.

That's where authenticity lives and trust thrives.

And when you've built that trust, the next time you do ask for the sale, people listen.

THE TRUTH DOESN'T JUST SET YOU FREE, IT MAKES YOU RICH

There's a reason some of the fastest-growing brands today sound nothing like their competitors.

They're not necessarily cheaper.

They're not always better.

But they feel real.

People don't just buy from them.

They root for them.

They read their emails. They tell their friends. They stay.

And it's not because those brands found a new funnel hack.

It's because they made a simple, powerful decision:

"We're going to sound like us. And we're going to tell the truth. Even when it's messy. Even when it's boring. Even when it's not optimized."

If you can make that decision, and stick to it, you won't need to shout.

You won't need to beg.

You won't need a hundred ads just to move the needle.

You'll have something better: a brand that people believe.

NOW TAKE ACTION

You've made it to the end of *The Hidden Code of Marketing*, and that already says something about you. You're not chasing hacks or hype. You're here because you believe honesty, transparency, and trust can actually sell better than fake urgency ever could. And you're right.

You've seen how brands like Domino's, Ben & Jerry's, and countless others turned things around not with tricks, but with truth. Now it's your turn.

Authenticity doesn't need a grand rebrand. It just needs a first step.

Maybe that's rewriting a pitch so it sounds like a person wrote it.

Maybe it's sharing a behind-the-scenes post about what you're learning, not just what you've perfected.

Whatever it looks like for you, do it today, not when your messaging is "ready," but while it's honest.

You already have the framework: clarity, consistency, and congruence.

You can use them as your compass whenever you write, speak, or sell.

If your words match your values and your promises match your actions, you're already ahead of most brands out there.

The brands that win tomorrow will be the ones that mean what they say, every single time.

So start now.

Say less, mean more, and build the kind of trust no competitor can copy.

Sincerely,

P. Sharma

for Reading My Book

Thank you for spending your time with The Hidden Code of Marketing.

I hope it's inspired you to rethink how you connect, communicate, and build trust with your audience.

If this book sparked a few ideas, or even challenged the way you approach marketing, I'd love to hear about it. You can reach me anytime at *panda@leadspanda.com.* Your stories, questions, and feedback help shape future editions and keep this conversation real.

And if you found value in these pages, please take a moment to leave a quick review on Amazon. It helps other marketers discover the book and join this journey toward more honest, human brands.

Thanks for reading, and for choosing to build something real.

~ P. Sharma

GET EXPERT HELP WITH YOUR BRAND STORY

If this book got you thinking about how your brand shows up in the world, great. That's where the real work begins.

At **LeadsPanda**, we help businesses tell their stories with honesty and clarity without losing their voice in the process. The result is marketing that's easy to create and built to work.

Whether you're reworking your website, planning your next campaign, or trying to sound more like *you* again, my team and I would love to help.

You can book a free consultation at

leadspanda.com/consult

for a friendly chat about what's working, what's not, and how we can make your message more real.

Let's make marketing something you're proud of.

NOTES

INTRODUCTION

1. Outlier Growth, Brian O'Conner, "Domino's turned complaints into $11B", https://www.outliergrowth.com/p/dominos-customer-feedback
2. Domino's Pizza, "Domino's® Pizza Turnaround", https://www.youtube.com/watch?v=AH5R56jILag
3. r/marketing, "Do any other new marketers hate realising how fake everything is?", https://www.reddit.com/r/marketing/comments/14s36bj/do_any_other_new_marketers_hate_realising_how/

1. WHY AUTHENTICITY BECAME NON-NEGOTIABLE

1. TIME, Daniel D'Addario, "Why the Kendall Jenner Pepsi Ad Was Such a Glaring Misstep", https://time.com/4726500/pepsi-ad-kendall-jenner/
2. USA Today, Brett Molina, "Burger King UK under fire for tweeting 'Women belong in the kitchen' on International Women's Day", https://www.usatoday.com/story/money/2021/03/08/burger-king-uk-under-fire-women-belong-kitchen-tweet/4627505001/
3. Edelman, 2019 Edelman Trust Barometer Special Report -"In Brands We Trust?", https://www.edelman.com/sites/g/files/aatuss191/files/2019-06/2019_edelman_trust_barometer_special_report_in_brands_we_trust.pdf
4. Edelman, 2023 Edelman Trust Barometer- "The Collapse of the Purchase Funnel", https://www.edelman.com/sites/g/files/aatuss191/files/2023-06/2023%20Edelman%20Trust%20Barometer%20Special%20Report%20The%20Collapse%20of%20the%20Purchase%20Funnel%20FINAL.pdf
5. Edelman, "The Collapse of the Purchase Funnel", https://www.edelman.com/sites/g/files/aatuss191/files/2023-06/2023%20Edelman%20Trust%20Barometer%20Special%20Report%20The%20Collapse%20of%20the%20Purchase%20Funnel%20FINAL.pdf

2. WHAT AUTHENTICITY ACTUALLY MEANS

1. Business Chief, Kate Birch, "Forrester Predictions 2023 says trust will be top priority", https://businesschief.com/leadership-and-strategy/forrester-predictions-2023-says-trust-will-be-top-priority
2. Notion, "The AI workspace that works for you.", https://www.notion.com/
3. Mailchimp, "We lost this page", https://mailchimp.com/404/
4. Ben & Jerry, Nikita Richardson, "I Dough and Dough: Ben & Jerry's Renames Classic Flavor to Celebrate Same- Sex Marriage", https://www.fastcompany.com/3047967/i-dough-i-dough-ben-jerrys-renames-classic-flavor-to-celebrate-same-sex-marriage
5. Liquid Death, About Us, https://liquiddeath.com/en-in/pages/manifesto
6. Ryanair, "Employee of the month", https://www.instagram.com/p/DLfV0OuOkO_/?hl=en
7. Huit, Organic Denim Leave your Mark. Make them Yours, https://hiutdenim.co.uk/pages/about
8. Bombas, We're Bombas, https://bombas.com/pages/about-us
9. JPI, Tom Brant, "Volkswagen emissions scandal dampens automotive industry credibility", https://jpinyu.com/2015/09/23/volkswagen-emissions-scandal-dampens-automotive-industry-credibility/
10. Shein, Our Impact, https://www.sheingroup.com/our-impact/
11. Yale Climate Connections, Sachi Kitajima Mulkey, "Shein is officially the biggest polluter in fast fashion", https://yaleclimateconnections.org/2024/09/shein-is-officially-the-biggest-polluter-in-fast-fashion-ai-is-making-things-worse/

3. THE PSYCHOLOGY OF TRUST

1. PubMed Central, Adrianna Jenkins, Lusha Zhu, Ming Hsu, "Cognitive neuroscience of honesty and deception: A signaling framework", https://pmc.ncbi.nlm.nih.gov/articles/PMC5042136/
2. Turning Data into Wisdom, Kevin Hanegan, "Harnessing Neuroscience and Psychology for Smarter Decision-Making", https://www.turningdataintowisdom.com/artsciencedidm/
3. Edelman, 2023 Edelman Trust Barometer - "The Collapse of the Purchase Funnel", https://www.edelman.com/sites/g/files/aatuss191/files/2023-06/2023%20Edelman%20Trust%20Barometer%20Special%20Report%20The%20Collapse%20of%20the%20Purchase%20Funnel%20FINAL.pdf

4. Neuromarketing, Roger Dooley, "Mirror Neurons and Sales Style", https://www.neurosciencemarketing.com/blog/articles/mirror-neurons.htm
5. Chobani, Chobani is Shaping the Future of Food, https://www.chobani.com/
6. Thought Economics, Dr. Vikas Shah, "A Conversation with Hamdi Ulukaya, Founder and CEO of Chobani", https://thoughteconomics.com/hamdi-ulukaya/
7. CNBC, Megan Graham, "Burger King faces backlash after linking ad campaign to mental health, showing the risks of cause-based marketing", https://www.cnbc.com/2019/05/03/burger-king-faces-backlash-after-linking-ad-campaign-to-mental-health.html
8. Verywell Mind, Kendra Cherry, "Mere Exposure Effect: How Familiarity Breeds Attraction", https://www.verywellmind.com/mere-exposure-effect-7368184

4. HOW TO MAKE YOUR BRAND MORE AUTHENTIC

1. Harvard Business Review, "Chobani Founder Hamdi Ulukaya on the Journey from Abandoned Factory to Yogurt Powerhouse", https://hbr.org/2022/04/chobani-founder-hamdi-ulukaya-on-the-journey-from-abandoned-factory-to-yogurt-powerhouse

5. AUTHENTIC FUNNELS THAT CONVERT

1. KInfield, "This is your friendly reminder to put your sunscreen on", https://www.instagram.com/p/C4YEFTxuozH/?hl=en
2. Goodr, Active Sunglasses for Anyone, https://goodr.com/
3. Blume, Make Every Day a Healthy Skin Day, https://www.blume.com/
4. BarkBox, Dog Joy, Delivered Every Month, https://www.barkbox.com/
5. Dove, Dove Real Beauty Sketches, https://www.dove.com/us/en/campaigns/purpose/real-beauty-sketches.html

6. KEEPING IT REAL IN THE AGE OF AI

1. Smart Insights, Dave Chaffey, "How can I use ChatGPT for marketing?", https://www.smartinsights.com/managing-digital-marketing/marketing-innovation/how-can-i-use-chatgpt-for-marketing/

2. HubSpot, Caroline Forsey, "The State of Generative AI & How It Will Revolutionize Marketing [New Data + Expert Insights]", https://blog.hubspot.com/marketing/state-of-generative-ai
3. HubSpot, "AI Trends for Marketers", https://offers.hubspot.com/ai-marketing

7. THE ROI OF BEING REAL

1. Duolingo, The free, fun, and effective way to learn a language!, https://www.duolingo.com/
2. Duolingo, "We believe in transparency and wanted to share this heartbreaking update.." (TikTok)
3. Duolingo, "Duo's streak on earth has ended but not his legacy." (TikTok)
4. Patagonia, "Don't Buy This Jacket, Black Friday and the New York Times", https://www.patagonia.com/stories/dont-buy-this-jacket-black-friday-and-the-new-york-times/story-18615.html
5. Death Wish Coffee, "Me to me: It's time to step it up.", https://www.instagram.com/p/DIMDKbltwXM/
6. Kickstarter, Brooklinen: All the quality, only a fraction of the price, https://www.kickstarter.com/projects/890193903/brooklinen-all-the-quality-only-a-fraction-of-the

ACKNOWLEDGMENT

Writing a book about authenticity has a way of testing your own. Every chapter of *The Hidden Code of Marketing* made me pause, question, and rewrite until the message felt honest. And I couldn't have done that alone.

To my family, thank you for giving me the space to think, create, and sometimes vanish behind a screen for hours. You reminded me that truth begins at home.

To the LeadsPanda crew, thank you for bringing your sharp minds and open hearts to this project. You turned late-night brainstorms into breakthroughs and reminded me that creativity doesn't happen in isolation.

To the clients and collaborators who let us peek behind the curtain of your brands, thank you for your trust. Every campaign, every experiment, every honest conversation taught me something about courage and connection.

And to you, the reader, thank you for giving this book a few hours of your life. If it helps you write, market, or lead with a little more truth, then it's done its job.

Here's to building something real.

ABOUT THE AUTHOR

P. Sharma, founder of LeadsPanda, is an entrepreneur passionate about cracking the code on what makes businesses thrive. His work has appeared in TechCrunch, Social Media Examiner, Business Insider, and Economic Times. For over a decade, he's worked with startups to global giants, crafting strategies that spark connections, skyrocket sales, and build unstoppable companies. When he's not diving into data or closing deals, he shares practical tips to inspire growth.

leadspanda.com

OTHER BOOKS YOU MIGHT LIKE

The One-Hour Street Smart MBA on

Email Marketing Metrics

The One-Hour Street Smart MBA on

Writing Click-Worthy Headlines

Check all our books at

leadspanda.com/books

Printed at Repro India Ltd.